"With all your science can you tell how it is,
and whence it is, that light comes into the soul?"

~ Henry David Thoreau

Also, by Cynthia Pitman

The White Room

Blood Orange

Breathe

BROKEN

Poems by

Cynthia Pitman

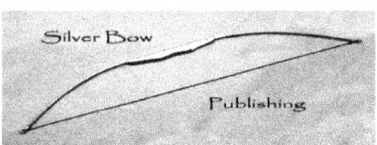

720 Sixth Street, Box # 5
New Westminster, BC
CANADA V3L 3C5

Broken - *Cynthia Pitman*

Title: BROKEN
Author: Cynthia Pitman
Cover Art: "Broken" painting by Tom Pitman
Layout and Editing: Candice James
© 2025 Silver Bow Publishing
ISBN: 97817740333791 softcover
ISBN: 97817740333807 e-book

All rights reserved including the right to reproduce or translate this book or any portions thereof, in any form except for the use of short passages for review purposes, no part of this book may be reproduced, in part or in whole, or transmitted in any form or by any means, electronically or mechanically, including photocopying, recording, or any information or storage retrieval system without prior permission in writing from the publisher or a license from the Canadian Copyright Collective Agency (Access Copyright).

© 2025 Silver Bow Publishing

Library and Archives Canada Cataloguing in Publication

Title: Broken / poems by Cynthia Pitman.
Other titles: Broken (Compilation)
Names: Pitman, Cynthia, author.
Identifiers: Canadiana (print) 20250251884 | Canadiana (ebook) 2025025493X | ISBN 9781774033791
   (softcover) | ISBN 9781774033807 (Kindle)
Subjects: LCGFT: Free verse. | LCGFT: Poetry.
Classification: LCC PS3616.I83 B76 2025 | DDC 811/.6—dc23

Broken - *Cynthia Pitman*

to beloved lifelong friends,
Chuck and Kerry Harmeling
and their wonderful family

Broken - *Cynthia Pitman*

Table of Contents

Authenticity / 1
To Dance in the Wild / 2
Downriver / 3
Ars Longa / 4
The Glassblowers / 5
In the Deep / 6
The Plight of the Evergreen / 7
The Thrifters / 8
The Lost Poem / 9
Squirrel Haven / 10
The Seed / 11

Hurricane Helene, 2024
    i. Hurricane Watch / 12
    ii. Hurricane Warning / 13
    iii. Landfall / 14
    iv. Appalachian Aftermath / 15
    v. Inland Florida / 16
    vi. Recovery in the Appalachians / 17
    vii Renewal / 18

Prison Sky / 19
The Stranded Prophet / 20
The Landscape Artist / 21
Buried Treasure / 23
Weeping Willow / 25
Broken / 26
Pretty Little Flowers / 27
Precipitation of the Soul / 28

The Disturbed Mind: Living with Mental Illness
    i. The Predator and the Prey: Depression / 29
    ii. The Watcher: Paranoid Anxiety / 30
    iii. Ghost: Derealization / 31
    iv. The Lacemaker: Psychotic Break / 32
    v. The Party Guest: Psychosis / 34
    vi. The Butterfly: Trauma – Dissociation / 35
    vii. Old Sorrows: PTSD- Flashbacks / 36

Truth / 37
The Lost Chord / 38
Spiritus Mundi / 39

Broken - *Cynthia Pitman*

To Seek, To Find / 40
Light / 41
A Red-Winged Bird / 42
Night Skating / 43

Making Do: The Art of the Mundane
    i. Homespun / 44
    ii. Ironing / 45
    iii. Cooking / 46
    iv. Laundry / 47

The Music of Our Home
    i. Blessed / 48
    ii. Cloudy Day / 49
    iii. Feeding the Birds / 50
    iv. Nighttime Concerto / 51

The Visionary and the Blue Mist: Into the Akashic Plane / 52
Danse Macabre: Life as Stained Glass / 57
The Earthen Jar / 58
Seashells / 59
When the Time Comes / 60
Night Closes In / 61
The Book of Gestures / 62

Acknowledgments / 65
Author Profile / 67

Authenticity

I set my scalpel to the page
and carve my identity
down to the bone,
until all that is left of me
is skeletal authenticity.
I discard the soft flesh
of my deceits into a trash heap,
then set it afire.
Ashes spiral up to the sky,
darkening the world.
Wild wind blows the ashes,
obscuring all sight,
but cleansing me to such purity
that I am hidden no more:
my bare bones rattle
with truth's delight.

To Dance in the Wild

This place is no place for me.
I live in a world of magical spells.
A place this devoid of mystical alchemy,
this laden with pain and human misery,
has little of what I need.
None of my sweet imaginings can make it
a haven for the likes of me.
It reeks of reality.
Those who do battle here
have strength, have resolve.
They know how to put their backs
into their work,
to bear down,
to sweat until it hurts.
I, instead, dither with a dream's delight
to see the unseen,
to avoid the fight.
I only long to see what I want
and think what I please,
to run against the wind
barefoot on cushioning clover
to dance in the wild.

Downriver

Thickets of palmetto trees
clench the riverbanks.
Water oaks rise,
dripping tangled curls
of Spanish moss.
My paddles slice the water
as if it were sweet syrup.
Barely a sound – just a quiet splash
as each paddle dips in
then emerges from the dark depths.
The canoe moves slowly,
sliding smoothly downriver.
Waiting somewhere there
is the respite I seek
from the metal and mortar
and crowds and heat
that surround me daily
as I pretend to live my concrete life.
All of its hard solidity
pinches me in on myself,
squeezing my breath from me
as I sweat away any hope of peace.
Only downriver will I find
cool water that reflects with clarity
the greenery and grace
that exists there to embrace me.
When I arrive there and breathe air
that is fresh and free,
life will stir again within.

Ars Longa

    to Isaac Harmeling

The weary artist, long unknown,
made his way down the hidden path
to the forbidden lake.
There he abandoned his brushes
on the shore
and knelt by the water's edge
to rinse his pallet one last time.
As the colors began to spread,
the still water began to boil and swell
with the thick multicolored pigments
until it was like kaleidoscopic lava.
This versicolored spectrum,
reflected in the sky above,
surrounded the artist
in a panoramic frenzy of saturation.
He stood a moment,
then dove into the water
and began to spin and spin and spin.
He rose again,
and slowly went ashore.
He gathered up his brushes and pallet
and left, stained in every hue.
Ever after, to his art he was true.

The Glassblowers

Inside the abandoned uranium mines
fires burn white hot and high.
Painted Glassblowers,
slathered in holy oil and sweat,
spin molten sand into sparkling light.
Shadows and light play
against their skin.
It crawls.
They add the rich blue of cobalt
dug from the earth's crust,
and the thick red of rubies
mined from the ancient caves.
Their breath shapes this colored glass
into beads and bands
that will adorn the Oracle
and her handmaidens.
Gold, wrested from the Alchemist's
fretful dreams, mixes with the molten sand
and swells from the Glassblowers' breath
into precious vessels.
The Priests come, and from these vessels
they drink the elixir of blood red wine,
a potion slowly fermented
in the deep tunnels of the mountain.
They savor its taste,
seasoned by the salty sweat
dripped into the vessels
by the Glassblowers.
Feverish, they mumble their incantations.
Then – all is quiet.
Slowly, the Priests retreat into the dark
and return to where their dark paths
take them.
The Glassblowers spin their blowpipes
and begin again
to breathe beauty into the world.

In the Deep

The fishes hide their beauty
in the dark.
No one is there to shine a light
upon them and endow them
with wondrous glory.
They swim in the deep,
indifferent to what beauty
surrounds them.
Their colors swirl with the current
as they wind their way
through the cold.
They pay no mind,
intent on only one thing:
feeding.
The beauty of their world –
and what they bring to this beauty –
eludes them.
They seek only sustenance.
They have no aesthetic
that yearns for beauty,
no ego that assigns it so arbitrarily,
no desperation that values it so deeply.
They have no envy.
But without beauty,
neither do they have joy.
Only the cold dark deep
of their cold dark lives.

The Plight of the Evergreen

In the fall, the staid magnolia
with her deep green leaves
envies the stately pied oak.
She stands peahen to his peacock,
her autumn leaves
turning a fungal funereal brown
next to his outstretched branches
arrayed in orange and red grandeur.
Even the magnolia's
lushly fragrant flowers
cannot compensate
for her dull fall robe
or compare to the dying oak's
vibrant merriment.

Winter will come.
The dreary magnolia
will turn the same green again,
while the oak's regal robe
cracks brown and falls to the ground,
a victim of winter's high tragedy.
But even then, as he rains death,
he will stand tall,
bearing black bare branches
that herald the end of fall.
In the oak's mighty winter shadow,
with his dark, stark branches
slicing the sky,
the magnolia will still wear
her same old verdant sheen –
she's only, after all,
just an evergreen.

The Thrifters
        to Jacob Harmeling

Look down.
Watch the ants on the ground
carry back to their mound
the cracker crumbs
we so carelessly dropped.
They hoist each one on their backs
and in single file
make their way to the hill
where each will eat its fill
and live another day.

What treasures we so cavalierly
toss away, treasures that are
often stolen away by the artist
who sees what we do not
and stows them away.
Someday the artist's hands
will grip the straight bars of debris
and twist them into a double helix
made from beauty's DNA.
Material is forged and bent,
shaped with intent,
then sent aloft
to touch the sky.

So let us fritter away
the gifts we are given.
Someone is always watching,
ready to salvage our casual debris.
Our excess can often be
art's one necessity,
our waste at times
its saving grace.

The Lost Poem

I know this cave.
I remember its striated stone walls.
Those must be my bones over there.
Once, before time, I sharpened rocks
and carved my words
into those walls.
Now, trapped here in the present,
I rub my hands over the words
but can discern no meaning
from the quasi-mosaic I once created.
I can only watch the walls
sweat rivulets into the grooves
that drip to the floor,
inch their way
to the pool beside my feet,
empty into the stream
outside the cave opening,
travel with it to the river,
and flow into the sea.
There the shape of my words
is lost forever
to the darkness of the deep.

Squirrel Haven
    to Kerry Harmeling

Past the secret casita
tucked behind the trees,
I follow a well-worn path
to a sculpted iron gate
flanked by coquina walls.
Here I enter the peace
of the shaded clearing.
Beside the sky-high bamboo stalks
is a freshly painted wooden ramp
that leads to the porch.
With lights strung around,
playful sculpted animals
crawling up the walls,
and a view to the placid lake
that fosters jumping fish
and welcomes diving birds,
this porch is a sacred space.

I sit down in the low-slung chair
and listen to the silent sounds
of so many memories made here:
the sweet words of friends' reunion,
the delighted cries of children
hugged by frames of photographs,
taco salad and laughter around a table
piled high with spicy condiments,
a bottle of Sparkling Peach Bellini
bubbling in a toast to old friends.
These memories are held tight,
embraced and kept safe
by the moss-draped trees
and my grateful heart.

The Seed

Born with a unique seed inside
passed down by her father,
the gardener's daughter made her way
through the landscape of life.
The seed germinated, sprouted,
and slowly grew throughout.
But choked by the eruption
of the world's corruption and lies,
the seedling died.
The fertile space
it had generated within her
became but a hollow place.
Lacking even the energy to fear
when smothered by the world's lava
and covered with its ashes,
she was but a victim
in her own private Pompeii.
No archaeologists came
to fill her empty space
with a cast of plaster
and show all the world
her own little disaster.

Hurricane Helene, 2024

(Based on true events)

i. Hurricane Watch

Raindrops wrinkle the river.
Soft waves gently slap
the sand where I stand.
The trees around me
whisper in the gentle breeze
that will soon grow
into a wild wind.
I stare across the expanse.
A lone boat heads home.
The quiet trembles.

ii. Hurricane Warning

The rain is falling harder now.
A steady pounding on the ground
by water-swollen pellets
sounds like bullets
pouring down on us.
I stand in the screened porch and look out
while being sprayed by mist.
The heavy raindrops
hit the river hard;
the water seems to boil.
Tree branches
sway in the building wind.
The slate gray of the sky
emits a low rumble,
and the ground has turned
to mud and mush.
Standing here, trapped by fear,
it seems as if the sun
has never shined
and never again will.
Knowing what is coming,
I realize things are going
to get very worse, very fast.
I lock the screen door,
as if that will help.
I know I must go in –
I hear the baby crying –
but I can't break the grip
of this scene.
I can only stand still
and stare.

iii. Landfall

flickering lights
total darkness
hold tight to the baby
hold tight to the baby
pounding rain
flashing lightening
howling wind
tree crashing thud
hold tight to the baby
hush little baby
house shaking
floor tilting
wood grinding
flood water seeping
hush little baby
mommy's here
rushing water
rattling windows
shattering glass
hold tight to the baby
please God help us
hold tight to the baby
please God please God

iv. Appalachian Aftermath

Houses that once stood
high on the mountain, tall and proud,
are splintered and smothered
by mudslides now,
their contents swept downstream
by the flooding brown water
to form makeshift dams,
life's treasures now but mere debris.
Age-old trees were nothing
but playthings, uprooted and smashed
into whatever was in their path.
Twisted train tracks stab the embankments.
Bridges are washed away by the floods,
taking cars and trucks with them.
Roads are gouged and eroded,
yawning gaps carved into the hills
in their place.
Downed powerlines drape across the ground,
some sparking, most dead.
Rescuers, gripped by fear,
shocked by the devastation,
plead to the TV cameras for more help.
Reporters shake
as they hold microphones
to survivors who, dull-eyed,
tell horror stories
in traumatized monotones:

The house was in the rushing water.
A rescuer was at the window,
taking the baby from the mother.
When he turned to help the mother,
the water swept the house away.
The mother was lost.

v. Inland Florida

This hurricane was indifferent
toward those living inland
in the Florida peninsula.
She barely deigned to show
her tailwinds' brushstrokes:
the gray glaring sky,
the black trees, mere silhouettes,
with their tangled swaying branches
and dark, dripping moss,
rain not really falling
as much as gathering in the air,
a smattering of water on the ground
reflecting the sky's glare.
She saved her real power to show
to those on the Gulf of Mexico coastline
and to those in the
Appalachian mountains beyond.
There she took her sweet time,
tearing roofs off of houses,
smashing what was left
into giant toothpicks,
uprooting trees,
crashing cars,
flooding towns,
downing power lines.
Those who survived
trudged through sludge and chaos,
searching helplessly for those who didn't,
while those who lived
in the inland peninsula
yawned and stretched,
enjoyed a hot cup of coffee,
then swept the leaves from the porch
and cleared away the debris.

vi. Recovery in the Appalachians

For months, the mountain people
have lived in tents, soaking in the mud.
Some are housed in campers.
Others live in cars and trucks.
No power.
No running water.
The government rejected
the sturdy "tiny houses"
the generous Amish made for free.
Something about no permits.
But the people are strong.
They help one another.
They know not to rely
on the government.
They know from experience
that this part of the country,
the South, will be ignored.
Churches – the ones left –
are the meeting places
for supplies, donations,
human connections.
The rumor here is that help
from the Army will now come.
Roads will be rebuilt.
Bridges will rise again.
Power will be restored.
Water lines will run clear.
The people are thankful but wary.
They shed no tears of relief.
They are hardened by experience.
They know, in their hearts,
they must rely on themselves.
They set their jaws,
grab their tools,
and dig in.

vii. Renewal

Sweet sunshine soothes
the sand made mud,
turning the sludge into
soft grit again.
It drinks the flooded water
into the air and transforms it
into cotton-ball clouds.
Gently, it pats dry
the green of the grass
and beckons the flowers
to unbow their stems
and gaze up again.
The blue sky,
shedding its fear,
creeps out from hiding
and restores its embrace
of the land.
The sun's dominion over the earth
is now steady.
The birds rejoice.

Prison Sky

Late Sunday mornings,
we leave off paying penance
and congregate in the prison yard
for the miracle:
the stars, imprisoned by daylight, escape.
They pierce the blue,
that shields them from mortal eyes,
and begin to shine again.
We marvel at this blue shimmering sky,
its stars so bright they blind our eyes.
Then the stars begin to fade behind blue.
The vision retreats.
Only the daytime sky remains.
We begin our slow silent walk
around the yard in awe,
humbled by how such stars
can so easily find freedom
from their bars of blue.

The Stranded Prophet

I carve my warning into the stone
with my own broken bones.
As night descends, no one comes.
I start a fire, stoke it,
watch the gray smoke curl higher,
and send signals with vaporous words.
No one sees them
except the night's eyes, the stars,
which tear up and turn blood red
as the smoke erupts.
Scattered around on the ground
lie brown brittle palm fronds,
wind-strewn by the wild storm.
I take one into my trembling hand
and etch a cryptic script into the sand
in a code only the moon knows.
But she and I both already know
I will always and forever
be stranded here alone.

The Landscape Artist

The boy went missing.
Only three years old
and lost in the primal wilderness
of the Appalachian Mountains.
His mother told the rangers
she only looked away for a minute,
just a minute, to take a photo
of the view from the trail
in the right light for her painting.
When she looked up, he was gone.
She called for him.
And called. And called.
And became more and more frantic.
The search teams came out –
rangers, police, hikers,
strangers, dogs, helicopters –,
and they all scoured the looming hills.
She was instructed to stay
at the spot where he disappeared.
The sounds overwhelmed her:
the shouting of his name by the searchers,
the flapping of the helicopters,
the barking of the dogs.
When night set in,
spotlights shone down from the helicopters
onto the dark, vast forest below.
On the third day they found
a single red sneaker, unlaced.
This find gave them hope.
But nothing came of it.
By day five the mother
could no longer stand it;
she picked up her canvas and began to paint.
For days more the helicopters
swept over endless miles
of shadowed peaks and valleys.
At night, their spotlights beamed down
only to be swallowed by the dark.
They searched the mountains

Broken - *Cynthia Pitman*

until the steep ground,
fierce with sharp, brittle brush,
finally drove them back.
After eight days the search
slowly tapered off.
By ten days, they were all gone –
all except his mother.
She pitched a tent and stayed,
returning only for fresh canvases.
The boy is a legend now.
The young hikers coming up the hill
don't know if the story is true or not,
but anyone serious about hiking the trail
respects the superstitions
of the Appalachian Mountains.
When they encounter the boy's mother,
her hair now gray and pulled back tight,
she is intent on her painting.
Her brush sweeps over the canvas.
No one speaks.
The hikers just leave her tokens for good luck –
food, water, flashlight batteries, blankets – ,
hoping these gestures will protect them
from being swallowed by the hills themselves.
She pays them no mind.
Then the hikers make their way up the trail,
and the old woman continues,
painting meticulous landscapes
of the scene before her,
including every stick,
every branch, every fallen leaf,
every piece of bark on every tree,
only to discard each finished painting
and begin again.
What no one knows
is that she always hopes
the next brushstroke
will reveal her boy's face.

Buried Treasure

I take the path through the woods
marked by the hickory tree.
Soon I stumble upon an old house
made of crumbling stone.
Beyond stretches a sheer white cliff
that towers over the ocean
as it spews rockets of foam
against the jagged rocks.
I think I lived here once,
years ago, when I was a young woman.
There – over there –
an engraved treasure chest wrapped in ivy
is buried there, next to that tree,
snuggled up to its roots.

When I step up on the front porch,
the cries of the rotting boards
sound like the cries I hear at night
in my restless sleep.
I creep into the front room.
The windows are closed, the curtains, drawn.
Dust shrouds everything
and muffles the noise of my rasping breath.
An old rocker sits by the fireplace.
I touch it gently and it begins to rock.
I think I sat here once.
I think I held the bundle of her
in my arms and sang to her.
I can hear the words.

I will stay here.
I will wipe the dust from the house,
wash and rehang the curtains,
open the windows,
and let in the fresh breeze.
There will be a clear line of sight
to the cliff.
This time I will hear –
not the mumblings of a full mind

Broken - *Cynthia Pitman*

overrun by dark memories and darker lies –
but her cries from the cliff
before she loses her grip.

The Weeping Willow

Without the willow,
how would the world weep?
The rains come in the spring,
but they wash the air clean,
so they are a joyful thing.
The wind moans and cries,
aches and sighs,
but sputters and coughs
and soon dies.
Snow settles softly on creation,
each perfect snowflake
a masterpiece in the making.
But once the sun shines down,
the snow is sacrificed
to the cold ground.
It is the arc of the willow,
its permanent bending low,
its supplication seeking mercy
that carries the weight
of the world's constant sorrow.
And permanent it must be,
for this world's sorrow
is deep, so deep,
and forever and ever
everlasting.

Broken

My bones ache,
full with emptiness.
I long to be lowered
into a bath of soothing nectar
from the wild honeysuckle.
I will vine to the sky
and sprout leaves of spring green.
From my vine will blossom
tiny, white-petaled flowers divine –
flowers with a pink-tipped kiss within
and with pollen-topped stamens
stained gold from an alchemist's rain.
When the wind stirs,
it will gently strum the stamens
like the strings of a harp
and carry far the sound
of a trembling bygone melody.
My vine will entwine
the cotton-puffed clouds.
From there, I will travel
the sea-blue sky
over the smoke-blue mountains
to the sky-blue sea.
I will float upon its tender eternity.

Pretty Little Flowers

Before they took her away,
I used to stand by my window
and watch my mother
work in her flower garden.
I can see her now, on her knees,
crouched down, spade in hand,
tilling yet another flower bed,
ready to bring color and life
into this saddest of worlds.

I watch her closely.
Then my chest tightens.
I see what she is doing.
One by one,
she plants her grandmother's
fine China teacups into the dirt,
their delicate handles pointing up.
With a curved hand,
she covers each cup with loose dirt.

Later, after I tell my father in fear
and they come to take her away,
she cries and clings to me,
explaining that she loved
the sweet little red flowers
on the cups, and had only wanted
to grow them in her garden.

Now, so many years later,
I gaze through the same window.
When the light hits the garden
at a certain slant at twilight,
I feel sure I see
sprouting from the weeds
fragile stems with tiny red blooms.

Precipitation of the Soul

A piece of plywood,
bleak-brown,
now covers the window
on the fourth floor.
I saw it all by happenstance.
Just a casual glance that way
and there she stood.
Seeking a final peace,
she must have thought
the window a portal
to the heavens' sweet release.

Now, when the memory
of her fatal flight
weighs heavy upon me,
I go to where I saw her last,
broken on the ground.
I lie there in her place.
I look to the morning dew
gathered around me.
I become one
with its quintessential essence –
its earth-bound wetness.
I curl myself into translucent
pearl drops and cling to the blades
of spring-green grass.
From there I evaporate,
rising to join the clouds
floating in the sky.
Fresh air caresses my mind,
soothing my cries.
The delight of sunlight
replenishes my spirit.
I then gather with the clouds
around me and rain down
to the ground again.
I rise, washed clean,
and am reborn into a new spring.

The Disturbed Mind: Living with Mental Illness

i. The Predator and the Prey: Depression

Agony prowls the streets tonight,
seeking easy prey.
My gnawing hopelessness
puts me at risk.
I have sought refuge,
but all doors have slammed tight.
Thus I, too, crawl the night.
From bin to bin,
I hide in the back streets,
but it detects my scent.
I know it is but a matter of time.
I howl at the moon. but she is cold
and does not answer.
I cry to the stars,
but they just blink indifferently.
The darkness that surrounds them
fears the light
just as I fear this night.
Without hope, I crouch
in an alley corner.
The cats resent my intrusion
and hiss a hiss of fierceness,
arching their backs
and baring their teeth.
Stray dogs growl.
Rats scurry.
At last, I surrender to agony.
At least it is familiar,
so it is my only hope
for some kind of peace.

ii. The Watcher: Paranoid Anxiety

She's a Peeping Tom of the soul,
an original voyeuse seeking evidence
of inner peace and happiness.
Those she meets toss her a smile
and she tosses back another smile –
but with a sneak peek deep into their eyes.
She surreptitiously struggles
to see if a light shines within,
illuminating contentment.
She has heard of such a thing,
but it is a stranger to her.
She wants just a quick look
to see if it is true –
that we can really live
without constant inner erosion
by dark fear and misery.
Or do we all wear a mask of lies?
She longs to lift her hand
and run her fingertips over the braille
of each new face, dig her nails in,
and see if she can peel back a mask
and maybe, happily, see real skin.
But she dare not.
She must maintain the mundane custom
of instead extending her hand.
But just a quick peek would be harmless,
and might someday reveal
that the face, in fact, is real.

iii. Ghost: Derealization

Lately I feel as if
I'm not here,
for when small talk erupts,
I hover between the lines,
and when I leave a place,
I leave behind no empty space,
as the air folds in on itself
behind me, like water,
so that no trace is left behind,
no carcass for casual
carnivores to pick clean
behind the scenes,
not even an ethereal mist
or a random memory.

iv. The Lacemaker: Psychotic Break

Over the steel door
of the cinderblock building
hangs a sign:
"Lacemakers Only."
Eyes ahead, without a sound,
we file in.
We take our seats.
The lock clicks.
All is silent.
But soon that blesséd silence
will be cracked by the incessant
clicking-clack, clickity-clack
of the carved ebony handles
of our spinning sticks.
The clock ticks.
We begin.
I wrap my hands around
the wooden handles and start to spin.
click
clack
clickity-clack
clicking-clack, clickity-clack
Scottish heathers begin to bloom
in the growing lace.
First comes the burst
of the soft lavender of Glencoe.
Then comes the sweet pink of the Highlands.
The last of the pattern
is the lime-green and gold of Arran Gold.
The beautiful heathers bloom in the lace
as the handles spin.
clicking-clack, clickity-clack
The pattern repeats.
clicking-clack, clickity-clack.
clicking-clack, clickity-clack.
The heathers bloom.
clicking-clack, clickity-clack
clicking-clack, clickity-clack.
With the beat of the clicks

Broken - *Cynthia Pitman*

of the spinning sticks,
I am soon spun into a trance. . .

I look down.
No longer are my hands spinning
the wooden handles.
Instead the thread comes from my palms,
sticky and thick, without need of a click.
I begin to spin the sinister thread.
No heather blooms from lace.
Now a deadly web appears.
I continue to spin again and again.
My web grows bigger and bigger,
menacing and thick.
I look around.
No one has noticed.
They all continue to spin.
clicking-clack, clickity-clack
One by one, I ensnare
each of the other lacemakers.
When captured, they struggle,
twisting and writhing,
only trapping themselves
tighter and tighter.
But the curséd clicking-clack, clickity-clack
of the wooden handles has finally stopped.
I can finally have peace
and rest my mind in blesséd silence.
Now if only the screams would stop.

v. The Party Guest: Psychosis

Spirals of copper wire
hang from the front porch eaves
of the old clapboard house in the woods.
Hanging from each are small bones –
of squirrels, rats, mice, birds,
whatever can be found loose in the woods –
painted different shades of blue.
On the porch floor
brushstrokes of red and yellow paint
trace the shadows made
by the full moon at midnight.
From the door hangs a wreath
made of honeysuckle vines.
Brown now, brittle and sharp,
they somehow still retain
the intoxicating scent of the flowers.

Inside, placed on straight-backed chairs,
sit store mannequins dressed in their finest:
jewel-colored satins and velvets,
draped in feathers and pearls.
This is where I go when
finally left deeply alone.
A chair is there for me.
I sit tall in it, straight-backed, like they do,
and listen quietly to the conversation.
Soon I begin to join in – slowly at first,
then stronger and quicker.
Faster and faster and louder and louder,
my words turn into screams
until I stand up, seize up, then fall.
Quiet now, covered in sweat,
I am lifted from the floor
and politely escorted to the door.

vi. The Butterfly: Trauma - Dissociation

The child cries out in fear,
then pain,
squeezes her eyes shut, tight.
She becomes a tiny butterfly.
Wings powdered with sunset lavender,
cornflower blue, and poppy red
spring from her shoulders
and spread.
She takes flight,
settling safely on the bookshelf
behind a bronze horse bookend.
He turns to look at her
and nods in recognition.
He snorts, neighs,
tries his best to cover the cries.
But she does not hear them.
She is too enraptured
by his beauty,
his soft mane and his shining coat,
his strong muscles.
She knows she is under his protection.
She is safe.
She falls asleep.
When she opens her eyes,
she is alone in her bed.
Her room is dark.
All is quiet.
She pulls the covers up
under her chin,
tucks her wings close
underneath her,
and hides her secret colors,
a fractured caterpillar
in her cracked chrysalis.

vii. Old Sorrows: Post-Traumatic Stress Disorder
–   Flashbacks

Here, downriver, in this hidden ossuary,
lie the bones of my old sorrows.
They used to walk with me
through my broken life.
I would care for them,
caress them, comfort them,
assure them I would never leave them.
But they covered themselves
with sharp skin, woven from nettles.
Their thorns pierced my palms
until they bled, a symbiotic stigmata.
I wept, but I could not let them go.

Once, though, when I crossed
this river with no name,
my old sorrows were washed away
downriver, and I was made new.
My palms healed.
I could breathe free.
But once in a while, when I am weary
and feel so all alone,
I come here and I stare
at the bones of my old sorrows.
I try to find peace here.
I must become reconciled
to the hard truth:
I will always bear
the scars of their wounds.

Truth

Under the spell
of the snake-headed shamanka,
the stranger began
to spread false prophecies
to the fallen people of the village.
But the sea formed a salty, gritty mist
that traveled to the village,
scrubbed clear the eyes and ears
of the villagers,
and burnt the lying tongues
of the shamanka
and the false prophet.
The people were thus left alone and free
to form their own understanding
of the world.
Realizing this, they wept.

The Lost Chord

The fallen angel,
broken,
stood alone upon the jagged cliff.
He opened his arms wide
and tried to sing the holy chord
that had been lost to him for so long.
Heaven opened its arms.
Thunder clapped.
Lightning split the sky.
The birds heard his words
and created a holy melody.
The trees bowed their branches
and offered their leaves
to the ruffling of the wind,
which sighed a soprano breeze.
A host of angels, clad in purest white,
softened the sky and sang sweet hosannas.
Together the world
raised its myriad voices
in everlasting euphony,
and sang the lost chord.
The fallen angel spread his arms,
fell to his knees,
and sang the chord in harmony.

Spiritus Mundi

The earth quakes, quivers,
rumbles underground.
Tectonic upheaval cleaves
a long crevice that splits the shell,
and the edges of this chasm
break into shards.
With a massive crack,
the earth gives birth:
a white-feathered bird
with a curved neck
emerges from the abyss –
a gathering of souls
that would be set free
from worldly misery.
It spreads its wings
and takes flight
as the shattered pieces
of its egg scatter into space.
Free of the bonds of gravity,
it spans the space of eternity.
The gathered souls sparkle
like a host of tiny stars.

To Seek, To Find
    to Chuck Harmeling

Hold a parable
in the palm of your hand.
Cup it gently.
Do not clutch it or squeeze it,
seeking simply meaning from it.
Scraping the skin of it
will not release
the anointing that awaits you.
Just a gentle curve of a cradling palm
will leave it open to the light
of the glorious sun.
Soon a sweet rain will shower down
and create shoots that spring forth
and burst with blooms of color and scent.
A holy pollen – the anointment –
will saturate the air that you breathe in.
From this nascent life,
understanding will grow.

Light

From beyond, darkness looms.
Not seen but felt, its tentacles
threaten to entwine me.
I spread my arms wide,
slide down the dew-dampened hill,
dive toward the horizon,
and crash into the hard sky.
I feel its cerulean blue
crack into pieces, each piece curled
like in a sunbaked lake bed.
My bones crushed,
I slide easily between the cracks
and glide into the dark universe
spotted with starlight.
I swallow the light of each bright star
until only I shine.
Now I am made full with light.

A Red-Winged Bird

A simple thing
like a red-winged bird
feeding on seed left for it
in a yellow wooden birdhouse
sends me into a deep reverie.
How often we exercise dominion
with kindness, giving sustenance
to living things that can give us
no reward but for the beauty
they bring us with their mere existence.
Our bond with them is a covenant,
a resistance to the void of space
and the threat of time.
Just a flash of a red wing
leads our eyes up
and is more than enough
to bring us to our knees
and humble us.

Night Skating

I slip out at night
and take my soul skating
on the frozen lake,
carving cryptic glyphs
into the ice that tell the stories
of the angels.
Opening my arms
and tilting my head back,
I gaze at the stars
that reflect their shine upon the ice.
I spin on one leg,
boring flumes into the ice
that spew effervescent spumes
into the sky.
I watch as the foam transforms
into white-winged angels.
Together we dance on diamonds
of reflected stars.
They then spread their wings
and fly high to the sky.
I circle the lake,
then stop and pull off
my skates.
I take one last look at the sky,
then walk home
through newly falling snow
that lands on my shoulders
soft and light,
like angel feathers.

Making Do: The Art of the Mundane

i. Homespun

The hand-stitched hem
of my home-made dress
is a little uneven.
The seam of the right sleeve puckers.
The back zipper buckles
and the pattern in the cloth
doesn't match up.
The bodice is too big,
the skirt too tight.
Loose threads here and there
shed everywhere.
The dress is a mess,
but I don't care.
It's mine. I made it.
And its little lavender flowers
with their tiny green leaves
make me feel wrapped
in the delicate scent of spring.

ii. Ironing

These white cotton dress shirts
need spray starch and steam.
I push my weight down hard
with my right arm
to smooth the wrinkles.
But the board has no pad –
just a worn cotton cover.
A pattern from the board's
zigzag metal surface
appears on the starched white shirt: .
crisscrossed diamonds
embedded in the cloth.
I worry at first.
This won't work.
But I grow to like them,
this myriad of diamonds
the steam creates.
They sparkle from the starch.
They are my art.

iii. Cooking

After supper, I go in the kitchen
all alone
and fix chocolate pudding.
I mix together hot bubbling milk
and Jello chocolate powder
in a pot on top of the stove.
When it stirs nice and thick,
I pour it into bowls.
Then I set the bowls
in the refrigerator to cool.
I haven't much patience.
I look in again and again,
trying to discern if the pudding
is cold yet, and ready to serve.

My patience gives out.
I pull the bowls from the cold
refrigerator and pass them out.
A thin chocolate skin
has formed on the top
of the pudding. I eat that first.
Then I eat the top layer,
cool and creamy.
But it is only when I get
to the bottom of the bowl
and taste the still-warm chocolate
nestled in the heart of the pudding
that I know I now know,
all on my own,
the secret alchemy of cooking.

iv. Laundry

I trudge to the cement-block building
across the parking lot,
lugging cracked plastic baskets
crammed full with the family's laundry
Filling the washers
with all the faded colors and dingy whites,
putting the quarters in the slots,
pulling the laundry out
after the washer stops churning,
putting it in the dryer
to spin and spin,
then pulling it out to fold –
all of these dreary tasks
make a dreary beginning
to the upcoming weekend.
But every Saturday morning, without fail,
when I pull the sheets from the dryer,
I gather them to my face
and breathe them in.
Then all my world
is warm and fresh and clean.

The Music of Our Home
    to my beloved husband, Tom Pitman

i. Blessed

A simple life.
Soft afternoons.
You there, in the other room,
napping.
Me here,
with my hot tea
and sweet imaginings.

ii. Cloudy Day

Smoke-gray clouds
shroud the day.
The mockingbird
in his ash-brown garb
swallows his song before
it can be heard.
Even the wind is still
and won't bother itself
to strum the windchimes.
The sky is selfish with sunlight.
All it will share is a white glare.
Today does not invite
a brisk walk outside.
Today is meant for the inside,
for the comfort of firelight,
warm brandy,
and your good company.

iii. Feeding the Birds

I watch you through the window
as you carry the bag of seed
to the birdhouse you built
so many years ago.
The squirrels on the ground below it
scatter, make an outraged clamor,
and scamper up the trees.
But they don't go far.
Nor do the birds.
Mockingbirds, redbirds, blackbirds,
the occasional dove –
they all take wing.
But they stay close, just out of sight.
You carefully fill the birdhouse with seed,
then scatter little piles around the base
so the squirrels won't have to wait
for what the birds spill.
Fifty years married,
and my heart is still touched
by your tenderness.

iv. Nighttime Concerto

Come. It is time now.
Let us leave behind
the burdens of this day
and retreat to the embrace
of the night.
Let us lie in her soft arms
and rock gently to the lullaby
of the music of our home.
The notes will float in the air
and caress our daily wounds.
Soon your hand will rest in mine
and we will smile in wonder
at the depth of our love.

The Visionary and the Blue Mist:
Into the Akashic Plane
to the Harmeling sisters, Franny and Lilah

My little sister has the Vision.
Born breach in a caul
at half-past midnight,
she was guided into the world
by the gnarled hands
of the old shaman-midwife.
When my sister wouldn't stop crying,
the shaman spun a spell
and gave her the dual gifts
of calm composure and second sight.
A third gift from the old woman
now sits on my sister's night table:
a jelly glass full of pretty pebbles.
Each night my sister selects certain pebbles
and forms a circle with them
on the floor between our beds.
She sits in the circle, quiet and still.
I sit in the middle of my bed,
just as quiet and just as still,
watching her:

She raises her arms
and summons the wind.
A gust blows through the window
and lifts the pebbles.
They circle around her head at arm's length.
She spins them into story-telling mosaics.
Her low voice mutters her prophecies:
how the young couple down the street
will find a cursed treasure
of silver coins in the basement;
how the strange woman up the hill
will have conjoined twins, one a mute;
how the shoemaker will lose his wife
then his family's shop after sixty years;
how a plague will come to the village

Broken - *Cynthia Pitman*

and fell the guilty and the innocent alike.
She is always right.

The plague chooses to come for her first:
Sweat. Pocks. Unquenchable thirst.
A cold cloth pressed on her forehead
turns limp and hot.
Aches. Cramping. Her legs won't stay still.
A foul syrup is forced into her mouth.
Heaving vomit, then nothing
but bile and blood.
Muscles loosen. Veins turn cold.
Darkness falls upon her,
around her, through her.
She is still.

I cried for a hundred years.
Now each night I am the one
to select pretty pebbles from the jar
and form a circle with them on the floor.
I sit within and spin and spin.
Darkness only. Then it lifts.
I see my sister in the menacing path
of the blue mist:

She has awakened and found herself
in a strange land.
She lies in a gray stone tower
upon a bed of sweet pea clover.
All about her are bright colors.
But from afar, the blue mist begins to crawl in.
It alters the colors with its ominous filter:
yellow daylilies are dulled into green,
pink bougainvillea become fuchsia,
the green leaves of the trees darken to black
and seem to hang too heavy,
the slate gray of the tower rocks turns a flat navy.
Even the sky is a different shade of blue;
more blue has intensified it
into an almost unbearable indigo.
My sister must be strong
if she is to reign here, for her reign

Broken - *Cynthia Pitman*

is what has been fore-ordained.
She will wear the crown
of dark blue sapphires.
All will bow down.

But the blue mist
has muddled her Vision.
What she does not see coming down
from the blue mountain beyond
is an army of armored soldiers,
wielding shining shields
and swords of steel.

Thick blue mist steams
and overlays the battle scene.
Clashing of steel.
Cries and screams.
Bright yellow fire flames into green.
Red life-blood mists into deep purple.
The battle ends.
The soldiers forge onward,
their bloodied swords sheathed,
their battered shields lowered.
The cries of the dying
left on the field
are for water, for succor.
The hallowed Mother
from the Blue Mist Mountains,
mystical, spectral,
fated to follow the blue mist
wherever it must go,
hears their cries, weeps,
and seeks to bring them relief.
Slowly crossing the field,
kneeling to tend to the fallen,
one by one, again and again,
she lays hands upon them.
The cries go quiet.
All is calm.
A soft wind blows

Broken - *Cynthia Pitman*

across the silent field.
All the ghosts are gone.
Darkness falls. Eons pass.
The mist clears:

My sister stands in the middle
of a wildflower field.
No longer does she wear
the sapphire crown.
The remnants she managed
to salvage from her doomed reign
are assembled at her feet.
She wraps the striped silk scarf
around her long blond curls
twirled in a circle atop her head.
She dons the white satin dress
and the cloak of ink-black cormorant feathers.
Her feet shod in doeskin,
she gathers one thousand brocade bags
she rescued from her stolen realm
and carefully stacks them
in the carved ebony wagon
she will pull behind her.
Then she sets out to every shore
to gather pebbles of every hue and tone.

When all the bags are full,
a thousand red-tailed hawks
congregate around her.
Each is given a brocade bag.
The hawks then take flight
and carry the gathered pebbles
to the deserted wildflower field
whence she has come.
There she meets them, empties the bags,
and sorts the stones by color and shade,
making a circular pebble palette.

She sits within the circle.
She knows I am watching her.
She can feel it, and so can I.

Broken - *Cynthia Pitman*

She raises her arms and summons the wind.

A gust lifts the pebbles.
She spins and spins
until story-telling mosaics
tell one hundred stories
of battlefield glories.
Her spun stories tell how this time,
it will be her armor and her shield
that are shining, blinding all other eyes.
This time, it will be she who wields
the sword of steel.
This time, it will be she who fells the foes
who seek the throne.

After her one hundred stories are told,
the pebbles fall to the ground.
She sits in spent rapture among them,
knowing now that her realm
will soon be recaptured.
Her stories will dispel the blue mist
and lay all strife to rest.
Her name will always be known:
she is my sister,
the Sovereign of Stones.

Danse Macabre: Life as Stained Glass

Years pass.
Night's sharp bristles
brush close: lead thistles.
The ending of life's light
shrouds all sight.
Naught is bright.
Edges grow thick:
life's leaded glass,
stained by the colors of strife,
is but shards soldered together
with swelling eternal night
closing in.

The Earthen Jar

I cradle against my breast
an earthen jar baked brown
in the noonday heat
then burnished a red-gold hue
by the burning sun.
This jar carries hoarded
effervescent flakes
of memories gathered
along the paths I have trod.
I seek a sand-grain expanse
with salt-sodden air
by a salty sea.
There will I strew the flakes,
seeds that will gestate,
break through their bed,
bud and bloom,
then flower my last days.
Scrubbed free of strife
by the grit of the sand,
their sweet scent will soothe
my trembling mind.
Petals painted soft pastels
will cover and close
my film-veiled eyes.
My going will be made gentler
by these memories ephemeral –
life's transient treasures,
their wealth gathered
and now, at the end, well-spent.

Seashells

The child I used to be
collected scalloped seashells
and buried them by the sea.
I close my eyes now,
a lifetime later,
and lie back in this sick bed
to watch her at her serious play:

Brow furrowed, she leans
to carefully collect each shell.
Turning it over and over again,
inspecting its shape and colors,
she either places it securely
in her red plastic pail
or tosses it back out to sea.
After her pail is full enough,
she settles on the sand cross-legged
and, with finger crooked,
digs a hole for each shell.
When she has safely buried them
deep enough, she packs the sand
and pats each little mound
with her confident hand.

Why did she bury these little shells?
Were they treasure to lay up
for another day?
Or did she plant them to grow
into a shell big enough
to live in, to hide in, safe, like a snail?
I'll never know.
But I think one day,
when I'm freed from this insidious bed,
I will float back to the sea.
Grown there will be memories
of life's beauty incandescent:
tiny Aphrodites draped in strands
of molten iridescent pearls,
rising resplendent from the shells.

When the Time Comes

When the time comes,
wash my hair in the fresh summer rain.
Brush it from my face
and let it hang in the new shining sun.
Anoint my skin
with the rich, dark oil
of the olives of Jerusalem.
Renew the chiseled grooves
that life has left.
Restore the flush
of life's first blush.
Soothe my weary feet
that have walked so far
for so very long
with clear water from the springs.
Wrap me in a cloak
made from soft white petals
of lily of the valley.
Let it comfort me within.
Then lay me in the arms
of heaven's sweet singing angels.
Let me rest there, forever,
in their feathered love.

Night Closes In

Smeared rain,
brushstrokes of mist,
shrouds dark mysteries
of the cryptic sky.
The night birds begin
to crowd the branches,
scrunched together,
hidden by the leaves.
Clouds of midges
swarm over the lake
and flutter nervously.
They know it is late.
Crickets croak
their night chorus.
Feral cats prowl.
I won't tarry.
I know my time is done.
I'm coming home.
It won't be long.

The Book of Gestures

The blind oracle,
unburdened by sight,
sits cross-legged at the foot
of the sacred forest pine.
Her spine grinds hard
into its dark bark
as she leans back
and murmurs a prayer.
She holds in her hands a holy book:
The Book of Gestures.
Bound in red silk and gold embroidery
dulled by eternity,
the book holds within it
blank pages wrought
from sacred wood shavings.
The oracle turns to the first page.
Upon this page and upon
each that follows it
she rests an open palm,
releasing her visions:

The artist sweeps a paintbrush
across the page, leaving a scene
of color and sheen.
On the page is a woman,
once broken but now healed
by brushstrokes that send her
vining and blossoming
upwards to the sky.

The musician strums an acoustic guitar –
first a major chord, then a minor,
then a run up the fretboard of the neck.
Joy and melancholy reverberate.
Hearts smile, then weep at the sound.

The surgeon with her scalpel
slices the patient's skin
and dips her instrument in.

Broken - *Cynthia Pitman*

With a few exact slashes,
a threat is removed
and a life protected.
A family rejoices,
sings hosannas.

The infant lies upon her back,
kicks her feet, and reaches high.
As her fingers find her feet,
she feels it in her toes.
At that moment she knows
that she alone is one entity
entire of herself.

The teacher lifts his arm
and points to a word on the board.
But the quiet child in the back
follows his finger and looks to the skies.
It is there her future lies.
He shows her the way.
He will never know she followed.

The dancer stretches then kicks her leg,
pointing it towards the sky.
She spreads her arms and twirls
round and round and round.
The world takes note and spins.

The astronomer twists the lens
on his telescope
and sees the rings of Saturn.
He is not content;
he twists again and again
to see the breadth of infinity.
The emptiness of space
is soon crowded with moons
and stars and planets and comets.
Black holes subsume themselves.

On every page, our stories are told.
Each of us reaches for eternity.
Each gesture we make

Broken - *Cynthia Pitman*

is but another attempt
to touch infinity.

But when the oracle turns to the last page,
the poet weeps, then swipes her pen
and writes what she fears ultimately happens
in all of our stories, to all of our lives:
"The End."

Acknowledgments

Academy of the Heart and Mind: *"Broken"*
Agape Review: *"The Lost Chord"*
Amethyst Literary Review: *"Light," "Night Skating,"*
"A Red-Winged Bird"
Boats Against the Current: *"Downriver"*
Bright Flash Literary Review: *"The Landscape Artist" (revised)*
Heart of Flesh Literary Journal: *"To Seek, To Find"*
Literary Yard: *"Ars Longa," "The Disturbed Mind: i – ii, iv-vi, "*
  "The Glassblowers," "Hurricane Helene, 2024: i – vii,"
  "In the Deep," "Making Do: ii – v," "The Prison Sky,"
  "Truth," "The Visionary and the Blue Mist: Into the
  Akashic Plane"
One Sentence Poems: *"The Disturbed Mind: iii. Ghost"*
  (published as "Ghost")
Parousia Magazine: *"Precipitation of the Soul"*
Soul Poetry, Prose, and Art Magazine: *"Authenticity,"*
  "The Plight of the Evergreen," "The Thrifters"
Spirit Fire Review: "When the Time Comes"

Broken - *Cynthia Pitman*

Broken - *Cynthia Pitman*

Author Profile

Cynthia Pitman, author of poetry collections The White Room, Blood Orange, and Breathe, has been published in Bright Flash Review, Amethyst Review, The Ekphrastic Review, Literary Yard, Boats Against the Current, Third Wednesday (One Sentence Poem finalist), Saw Palm: Florida Literature and Art (Pushcart Prize nominee), and others, and in anthologies Pain and Renewal, Brought to Sight & Swept Away, Nothing Divine Dies, and What is All This Sweet Work?

www.ingramcontent.com/pod-product-compliance
Lightning Source LLC
Chambersburg PA
CBHW071253070526
44583CB00017B/2456